chop, sizzle, & stir

chop, sizzle, & stir

easy recipes for fabulous **stir-fries**

Nadia Arumugam

photography by Richard Jung

RYLAND
PETERS
& SMALL

LONDON NEW YORK

Dedication

For Mummy, with love.

Design and photographic art direction
Steve Painter
Senior Editor Céline Hughes
Production Controller Toby Marshall
Art Director Leslie Harrington
Publishing Director Alison Starling

Food Stylist Sunil Vijayakar
Prop Stylist Róisín Neild
Index Hilary Bird

Author's acknowledgments
A warm thank you to the lovely folk at
Ryland Peters & Small, especially my most
favorite editor, Céline Hughes. To Richard
Jung and Sunil Vijayakar, thank you for
making my food look so delectable! For his
neverending appetite, I salute Peter, my
faithful guinea pig. And last but certainly
not least, thank you to my family.

First published in the
United States in 2009 by
Ryland Peters & Small, Inc.
519 Broadway, 5th Floor
New York, NY 10012
www.rylandpeters.com

10 9 8 7 6 5 4 3 2 1

Text © Nadia Arumugam 2009
Design and photographs
© Ryland Peters & Small 2009

Printed in China

ISBN: 978-1-84597-849-5

Library of Congress Cataloging-in-
Publication Data

Arumugam, Nadia.
  Chop, sizzle, & stir : easy recipes for fabu-
lous stir-fries / Nadia
Arumugam ; photography by Richard Jung.
    p. cm.
  Includes index.
  ISBN 978-1-84597-849-5
  1. Cookery, Asian. 2. Quick and easy
cookery. I. Title.
  TX724.5.A1A82 2009
  641.595--dc22

2008049310

Notes
• All herbs used in these recipes are fresh
unless specified as dried.
• All spoon measurements are level
unless otherwise specified.
• Ovens should be preheated to the
specified temperatures. All ovens work
slightly differently. We suggest you consult
the maker's handbook for any special
instructions, particularly if you are using
a convection oven, as you may need to
adjust temperatures accordingly.

contents

introduction

The joy of stir-frying is that as long as you have a pan, a cooking spoon, and a stove, you are all set to go! However, there are a few simple guidelines you can follow to ensure that you get the best out of your stir-fry.

You can use a large skillet for stir-frying, but the best choice is a wok. The curved sides provide a large cooking surface so that as many of the ingredients as possible get direct contact with heat—this enables them to cook quickly rather than stewing or steaming. Look after your wok! Before you use it, rub the inside lightly with vegetable or peanut oil, then plunge it in water and dry it. Repeat this three or four times. To clean it, never use detergent. Rinse it well with hot water and use a scouring pad to remove any stubborn remnants. Dry it well, then rub the interior with a little oil before storing.

To get that pleasing sizzle when the ingredients hit the wok, use vegetable, peanut, or sunflower oil, as they have high burning points and mild flavors. Avoid using olive oil for stir-frying because it burns at a relatively low temperature and can have a strong olive flavor that is incompatible with Asian cooking. Make sure the oil is hot before you throw in the ingredients.

Make life easy for yourself by preparing all your ingredients before you start cooking. Remove any excess fat from the meat, then slice or cut it into evenly sized pieces. If you have a very thick cut of meat, sandwich it between two sheets of plastic wrap and flatten with rolling pin until no more than ¾ inch thick, then cut as desired. To prepare vegetables, remember that those with a high water content, such as bok choy, will cook quicker than denser vegetables like carrots. Compensate for this by cutting the denser vegetables smaller, or by adding them to the wok first. If you are cooking with both meat and vegetables, first seal the meat in batches to prevent overcrowding the wok, which will cause the meat to stew in its own juices. Sear the meat until browned all over, then remove from the wok while you cook the vegetables. Return everything to the wok before adding any sauce at the end.

Whether there is time for a quick marinade, or you need dinner on the table in 15 minutes, you'll find a healthy, mouthwatering stir-fry here to make you look forward to your super-quick, super-satisfying weekday supper.

noodles & rice

Fat and chewy wheat-based Japanese udon noodles make for a wonderfully satisfying meal. The sauce gets its complex undertones from a good dose of oyster sauce and is absorbed by the tofu and meaty shiitake mushrooms for a thoroughly flavorful dish.

14 oz. fresh udon noodles

2 tablespoons vegetable oil

10 oz. firm tofu, cut into 1-inch cubes

1-inch piece of fresh ginger, peeled and shredded

3 scallions, white and light green parts cut into 1-inch lengths and shredded, and green parts sliced on the diagonal

1 red chile, seeded and shredded

7 oz. shiitake mushrooms, stalks discarded and caps sliced

Sauce

2 tablespoons oyster sauce

1 tablespoon light soy sauce

⅔ cup vegetable stock

1 tablespoon cornstarch, combined with 2 tablespoons cold water

Serves 2

udon noodles with tofu & shiitake mushrooms

Bring a saucepan of water to a boil. Throw in the noodles and cook according to the packet instructions. Drain and rinse under cold running water. Set aside.

Combine all the sauce ingredients in a bowl and set aside.

Heat the oil in a wok or large skillet until hot. Add the tofu in batches and stir-fry over high heat until golden all over. Remove the tofu from the wok and drain on paper towels.

Add the ginger, shredded scallions, and chile to the wok and stir-fry for 1 minute, then throw in the shiitake mushrooms. Cook for 1 more minute, then pour in the sauce and bring to a boil. Reduce the heat, return the tofu to the wok, and simmer gently for 1–2 minutes, or until the sauce has thickened.

Stir the drained noodles into the wok very carefully, then heat through until piping hot. Remove from the heat and divide between 2 bowls. Garnish with the remaining scallions and serve immediately.

Chow mein is a classic noodle stir-fry that should be part of every keen cook's repertoire. Treat this recipe as a basic guide to which you can add your own touches. Try varying the vegetables and replacing the beef with chicken or even tofu.

10 oz. sirloin beef or fillet, trimmed of fat and very thinly sliced

10 oz. fresh medium egg noodles

1½ tablespoons peanut oil

3 scallions, finely chopped, white and green parts kept separately

6 oz. choy sum (or bok choy), chopped into 1-inch pieces, stalks and leaves kept separately

1 red chile, thinly sliced, to garnish (optional)

Marinade

1½ tablespoons dark soy sauce

½ tablespoon Chinese rice wine

½ teaspoon sugar

1 garlic clove, crushed

1 teaspoon finely grated fresh ginger

2 teaspoons cornstarch

Sauce

2 tablespoons oyster sauce

¾ cup chicken stock

1 tablespoon light soy sauce

1 tablespoon dark soy sauce

2 teaspoons cornstarch

Serves 2

beef chow mein

Put the beef in a bowl, add all the marinade ingredients, mix well, and set aside.

Bring a saucepan of water to a boil. Throw in the noodles and blanch for 2–3 minutes. Drain and rinse under cold running water. Set aside.

Combine all the sauce ingredients in a bowl and set aside.

Heat 1 tablespoon of the oil in a wok or large skillet until hot. Add the marinated beef in 2 batches and stir-fry over high heat for 2–3 minutes, or until well sealed all over. Remove the beef from the wok and set aside.

Heat the remaining oil in the wok, then add the white parts of the scallions and stir-fry for just 30 seconds. Add the stalks of the choy sum and stir-fry for 2 minutes. Pour in the sauce and bring to a boil. Let bubble for 1 minute, then return the beef to the wok and stir through.

Stir the drained noodles into the wok, then cook for 1–2 minutes, or until the noodles are tender. Divide the chow mein between 2 bowls, garnish with the remaining scallions and the chile, if using, and serve immediately.

This refreshing salad gets its heat from the chili sauce and fresh ginger, sweetness from honey, tartness from lime juice, and saltiness from roasted peanuts. It is made with distinctive transparent glass noodles. Serve this dish as a light summer appetizer for four people, or for two as a sumptuous entrée.

Laotian pork & glass noodle salad

1½ tablespoons vegetable oil

2 small shallots, halved and thinly sliced

2 garlic cloves, crushed

1-inch piece of fresh ginger, peeled and finely grated

1 red chile, seeded and finely chopped

1 lemon grass stalk, outer skin removed and bottom 4 inches finely chopped

12 oz. ground pork

3½ tablespoons fish sauce

2 tablespoons Chinese rice wine or dry sherry

3 tablespoons chili sauce

freshly squeezed juice of 1 lime

3½ tablespoons honey

6½ oz. dried glass or cellophane noodles

a small bunch of cilantro leaves, roughly chopped

4 large iceberg lettuce leaves

¾ cup honey-roasted peanuts, roughly chopped

Serves 4 as an appetizer or 2 as an entrée

Heat the oil in a wok or large skillet until hot. Throw in the shallots and stir-fry over high heat for 2 minutes. Add the garlic, ginger, chile, and lemon grass. Cook for 2 more minutes until the garlic is golden.

Add the pork and stir to break up any lumps. Stir-fry until browned, then add the fish sauce, rice wine, chili sauce, lime juice, and honey. Simmer for 2 minutes, then remove from the heat.

Meanwhile, put the noodles in a large heatproof bowl and cover with boiling water. Soak for 3–4 minutes, or until softened. Drain and rinse under cold running water. Cut them into shorter strands with kitchen scissors.

Add the noodles to the wok and mix evenly through the pork mixture. Return to the heat and simmer for 3–4 minutes, or until the noodles have absorbed most of the liquid. Remove from the heat and stir in the chopped cilantro.

You can serve the salad hot, or let it cool to room temperature, then chill in the fridge for a few hours first. Serve in the lettuce leaves and garnish with the chopped peanuts.

Spicy and satisfying, this street-food favorite packs in all the flavors of Thailand. The shrimp paste adds a distinctive savory depth to the dish, so don't let its pungent aroma put you off. And don't forget the squeeze of lime at the end for that essential tangy finish.

chicken pad Thai

15 oz. dried flat Thai rice noodles

2 large garlic cloves, crushed

1 large red chile, seeded and finely chopped, plus ½, finely chopped, to garnish

1 teaspoon shrimp paste (optional)

1 tablespoon vegetable oil, plus extra if needed

2 skinless chicken breasts, cut into 1-inch pieces

2 tablespoons fish sauce

2 eggs, lightly beaten

1 cup bean sprouts

a small bunch of Chinese chives, cut into 1½-inch lengths

1 tablespoon tamarind paste

1 tablespoon palm sugar or light brown sugar

3 tablespoons chopped roasted peanuts

2 scallions, green and light green parts only, thinly sliced on the diagonal

a squeeze of fresh lime juice

2 tablespoons roughly chopped cilantro leaves, to garnish

lime wedges, to serve

Serves 2

Put the noodles in a large heatproof bowl and cover with boiling water. Soak for 20 minutes, or until softened but not cooked through. Drain well.

Meanwhile, put the garlic, chile, and shrimp paste, if using, in a pestle and mortar and grind until you have a rough paste. Alternatively, blitz in a food processor with a little water.

Heat the oil in a wok or large skillet until very hot. Add the paste and fry over high heat for 1 minute, or until fragrant. Season the chicken with ½ tablespoon of the fish sauce and add to the wok. Stir-fry for 4 minutes, or until just cooked through. Remove the chicken from the wok and set aside.

Heat another ½ tablespoon oil in the wok, if necessary. When hot, pour in the beaten eggs. Leave the bottom to set, then break up with a spoon to get softly set scrambled eggs. Return the chicken to the wok with the drained noodles, bean sprouts, and Chinese chives. Stir well.

Meanwhile, combine the remaining fish sauce with the tamarind paste and palm sugar, then add to the wok with half the peanuts. Stir-fry for 2–4 minutes, or until the noodles are tender. You may need to sprinkle in a little water if the noodles look too dry. Stir in the scallions and lime juice. Taste and add more fish sauce if you think it needs it.

Divide the pad Thai between 2 bowls, garnish with the chopped cilantro, chile, and remaining peanuts, and serve immediately with lime wedges.

In this stunning dish, the black sesame seed coating not only looks striking but its intense nutty aroma perfectly complements the meaty fish. Soba noodles are best served warm or at room temperature, as this allows all the delicious flavors in the dressing to meld and infuse the noodles. Shoyu and tamari are Japanese soy sauces, but if you can't get hold of either, simply substitute with dark soy sauce.

6 oz. dried soba noodles

½ teaspoon toasted sesame oil

2 teaspoons shoyu or tamari soy sauce

⅓ cup black sesame seeds

10 oz. tuna steak, cut into 1-inch cubes

2 tablespoons vegetable oil

Dressing

¾ teaspoon wasabi paste

2 tablespoons mirin (Japanese rice wine)

1 tablespoon rice vinegar

2 teaspoons shoyu or tamari soy sauce, plus extra if needed

½ tablespoon vegetable oil

1 garlic clove, crushed

¼ teaspoon finely grated fresh ginger

2 tablespoons thinly sliced nori seaweed sheets

Serves 2

warm soba noodles with black sesame seared tuna

Bring a saucepan of water to a boil. Throw in the noodles and gently push into the water as they soften. Cook for 4–5 minutes, or until tender but not soft. Drain and rinse under cold running water, then drain again well and stir in the sesame oil. Set aside.

Put the soy sauce in one bowl and the sesame seeds in another. Dip the tuna pieces in the soy sauce, then toss in the sesame seeds until evenly coated.

Heat 1½ tablespoons of the vegetable oil in a wok or large skillet until hot. Add the tuna pieces in batches and sear briefly over high heat so that they are still pink on the inside, just a few seconds. Remove from the wok and set aside. Clean out the wok.

To make the dressing, combine the wasabi with the mirin, vinegar, and soy sauce in a bowl and set aside. Heat the remaining oil in the wok until hot, then add the garlic and ginger. Stir-fry for 30 seconds, then reduce the heat and add the dressing. Stir well, then add the noodles and toss until piping hot. Remove from the heat and very gently stir the tuna pieces through the noodles.

Taste and add more soy sauce if you think it needs it. Let cool until warm, then divide between 2 bowls and garnish with the seaweed.

Sambal olek is a concentrated chili paste with a fiery kick. It is often used to enliven Indonesian dishes such as this punchy meat and vegetable fried rice and can be increased or reduced in quantity, depending on how much heat you like.

Indonesian fried rice

2½ tablespoons vegetable oil

1 small onion, finely chopped

2 garlic cloves, crushed

2 tablespoons sambal olek or chili sauce

2 teaspoons shrimp paste

1 large skinless chicken breast, about 8 oz., diced

6½ oz. uncooked shelled shrimp, roughly chopped

3½ oz. carrot, finely grated

6½ oz. canned corn, well drained

3½ oz. trimmed green beans, finely chopped

1 lb. cold, cooked basmati rice

1 tablespoon light soy sauce

2 large eggs, lightly beaten with a pinch of sea salt

Serves 4

Heat 2 tablespoons of the oil in a wok or large skillet until hot. Add the onion and stir-fry over high heat for 2–3 minutes, or until softened and golden. Add the garlic and continue to cook for 1 minute. Add the sambal olek and shrimp paste and cook for 1 minute, then throw in the chicken. Stir-fry for 2 minutes, then add the shrimp and cook until opaque and just cooked through.

Throw in the carrot, corn, and green beans and cook for about 2 minutes, or until the beans are cooked but still crunchy.

Add the rice and soy sauce to the wok and mix through. Cook until the rice is piping hot, then remove from the heat and set aside.

Heat the remaining oil in a large skillet and pour in the beaten eggs. Let set into a thin omelet. Transfer to a cutting board and let cool for 1 minute. Roll up the omelet tightly and slice as thinly as possible.

Divide the fried rice between 4 bowls and garnish with the slices of omelet.

This is a great way to transform pantry staples, rice and canned crabmeat, into a luxurious feast with the addition of a few fresh ingredients. If you are really looking to impress, then use freshly picked white crabmeat, but go easy on the flavorings, as you don't want to overwhelm the delicate sweetness of the crab.

1 tablespoon peanut oil

1 small onion, finely chopped

2 garlic cloves, crushed

1 large red chile, seeded and finely chopped

4½ oz. fine asparagus, cut into 1-inch lengths, stalks and tips kept separately

1 tablespoon light soy sauce, plus extra if needed

6½ oz. canned or fresh white crabmeat, well drained

1½ cups cold, cooked jasmine rice

1 tablespoon sweet chili sauce

¼ teaspoon toasted sesame oil

2 tablespoons snipped chives

Serves 2

wok-tossed jasmine rice with crabmeat & asparagus

Heat the peanut oil in a wok or large skillet until hot. Add the onion and stir-fry over high heat for 2–3 minutes, or until softened and golden. Add the garlic and chile and cook for a further minute. Throw in the asparagus stalks and stir-fry for 2 minutes. Add the asparagus tips and 2 teaspoons of the soy sauce and stir-fry for 30 seconds. Stir in the crabmeat and and cook over medium heat until heated through.

Mix in the rice, then pour in the chili sauce, sesame oil, and remaining soy sauce. Stir well until everything is thoroughly combined and the rice is piping hot. Taste and add more soy sauce if you think it needs it, then stir in the chives and remove from the heat. Divide between 2 bowls and serve immediately.

A plate of fried rice makes a lovely, all-in-one meal, but it can get a little boring, especially if you stick to the same old formula. Ring the changes, without any extra fuss, by adding some green curry paste and coconut milk for a Thai twist.

green curry fried rice
with chicken, green beans, & peas

6 skinless, boneless chicken thighs, cut into 1-inch pieces

2 tablespoons fish sauce, plus extra if needed

2 teaspoons finely grated fresh ginger

2 tablespoons vegetable oil

2 shallots, finely chopped

2 garlic cloves, crushed

¼ cup Thai green curry paste

¼ cup coconut milk

5 oz. trimmed green beans, cut into ½-inch lengths

1 cup peas

3 cups cold, cooked jasmine rice

a small bunch of cilantro leaves, roughly chopped

sea salt and freshly ground black pepper

thinly sliced red chile, to garnish (optional)

lime wedges, to serve

Serves 4

Put the chicken, half the fish sauce, the ginger, and a little black pepper in a bowl and toss until well mixed.

Heat the oil in a wok or large skillet until hot, add the shallots, and stir-fry over high heat for 2–3 minutes, or until softened and golden. Add the garlic and cook for 1 minute. Stir in the curry paste, then after 1 minute stir in the coconut milk. Cook over high heat for 2–3 minutes until the cream has reduced by half.

Add the chicken and stir-fry over high heat for 3–4 minutes, or until sealed on the outside. Add the green beans and stir-fry for 2 minutes. Throw in the peas and cook for a further minute until the vegetables are tender but still crunchy and the chicken is cooked through. Season with the remaining fish sauce.

Mix in the rice and stir until everything is well combined and the rice is piping hot. Season with sea salt or more fish sauce if you think it needs it and stir in the chopped cilantro. Divide between 4 bowls and garnish with chile, if using. Serve immediately with lime wedges.

vegetables

Transform everyday vegetables into a memorable meal with a few carefully chosen whole and ground spices. As in many Indian-influenced dishes, a spiky ginger and garlic paste forms the basis of this stir-fry. Why not make extra and keep in the fridge or freezer for another day?

1-inch piece of fresh ginger, peeled

2 garlic cloves, crushed

1 tablespoon vegetable oil

½ teaspoon fennel seeds

1 teaspoon cumin seeds

1 onion, halved and sliced

¼ teaspoon ground cumin

¼ teaspoon ground coriander

½ teaspoon ground red chile

⅔ cup canned chopped tomatoes

6½ oz. cauliflower, cut into small florets

2 carrots, cut into 1½-inch matchsticks

1 cup trimmed green beans, cut on the diagonal into 1½-inch lengths

2 tablespoons chopped cilantro leaves, to garnish

sea salt

cooked rice, to serve

Serves 2

spiced mixed vegetables with cumin & fennel seeds

Put the ginger and garlic in a pestle and mortar and grind until you have a rough paste. Alternatively, blitz in a food processor with a little water.

Heat the oil in a wok or large skillet until hot. Add the fennel and cumin seeds and stir-fry over high heat until they start to pop. Add the onion and cook for a further 3–4 minutes, or until golden. Stir in the ginger and garlic paste and stir-fry for a further 2 minutes. Spoon in the ground cumin, coriander, and red chile, and after a few seconds, the canned tomatoes. Cook over high heat for 1 minute, or until most of the liquid has evaporated.

Throw the cauliflower and carrot into the wok with a good sprinkle of water, stir, then cover and cook for 2 minutes.

Add the green beans, season with sea salt, and cook for a further 2–3 minutes, uncovered, until the vegetables are cooked but still a little crunchy. Taste and add more salt if necessary.

Remove from the heat and stir in the chopped cilantro. Divide between 2 bowls and serve immediately with rice.

This is a hearty and flavorful vegetarian dish traditionally eaten on the first day of Chinese New Year—Buddhists believe that meat should not be eaten on the first five days of the year. Every Buddhist family has their own version and ingredients vary from cook to cook. Here's my version.

Buddha's delight

½ teaspoon Chinese five-spice powder

8 oz. firm tofu, cut into 1-inch cubes

2 tablespoons vegetable oil

3 garlic cloves, crushed

6½ oz. small broccoli florets

6½ oz. miniature or baby bok choy, halved

6½ oz. snow peas

1 large carrot, cut into matchsticks

1 red bell pepper, seeded and cut into matchsticks

3 oz. canned water chestnuts, drained and sliced

3 oz. canned sliced bamboo shoots, drained and rinsed

cooked rice or noodles, to serve

Sauce

2 tablespoons oyster sauce

2 tablespoons light soy sauce

½ cup vegetable stock

1 tablespoon cornstarch, combined with 2 tablespoons cold water

Serves 4

Combine all the sauce ingredients in a bowl and set aside.

Sprinkle the five-spice powder over the tofu.

Heat the oil in a wok or large skillet until hot. Add the tofu in batches and stir-fry over high heat until golden all over. Remove the tofu from the wok and drain well on paper towels.

Add the garlic to the wok and stir-fry for 1 minute, or until golden. Add the broccoli, bok choy, snow peas, carrot, and red bell pepper with a sprinkle of water and stir-fry over high heat for 2–3 minutes. Finally, throw in the water chestnuts and bamboo shoots.

Pour the sauce into the wok and bring to a boil, then reduce the heat and simmer gently for 2 minutes, or until the sauce has thickened. Divide between 4 bowls and serve with rice or noodles.

stir-fried mixed mushrooms with chili bean sauce

Earthy mushrooms are given a boost of flavor with the pungent and complex aromas of chili bean sauce in this vegetarian stir-fry. Choose from any fresh Asian mushrooms in your local supermarket, such as shiitake, enoki, buna-shimeji, and oyster.

2 tablespoons vegetable oil

2 garlic cloves, crushed

½ red chile, seeded and chopped

4 scallions, white and light green parts only, sliced on the diagonal

14 oz. mixed Asian mushrooms, roughly torn or chopped into bite-size pieces

2 tablespoons chili bean sauce

1 tablespoon light soy sauce, plus extra if needed

Serves 2

Heat the oil in a wok or large skillet until hot. Add the garlic and chile and stir-fry over high heat for 1 minute. Add the scallions and cook for a further 30 seconds.

Add the mushrooms and stir-fry for 1–2 minutes. Combine the chili bean sauce and soy sauce in a bowl, then pour into the wok. Cook for 4–5 minutes, or until the mushrooms are tender and cooked through. Taste and add more soy sauce if you think it needs it. Serve immediately.

firecracker Chinese greens

This recipe gets its name from the punchy chile and tomato jam that the Chinese greens are cooked with.

1½ tablespoons vegetable oil

2 garlic cloves, thinly sliced

1 lb. 4 oz. trimmed Chinese greens, roughly chopped, stems and leaves kept separately

Chile jam

3 tablespoons sugar

2 tablespoons rice vinegar

½ tablespoon light soy sauce, plus extra if needed

2 small tomatoes, peeled, seeded, and chopped

2 large red chiles, seeded (if desired) and very finely chopped

½ teaspoon finely grated fresh ginger

Serves 4

To make the chile jam, put the sugar and 1 tablespoon water in a saucepan over gentle heat. Cook until the sugar dissolves, then turn up the heat and boil until light amber. Remove from the heat, pour in the vinegar and soy sauce, and swirl the pan. Be careful: the syrup will spit. Add the tomatoes, chiles, and ginger and return to the heat. Bring to a boil, then reduce the heat and simmer, stirring occasionally, for 5–7 minutes, or until thick and sticky. Set aside.

Heat the oil in a wok or large skillet until very hot. Add the garlic and stir-fry for 30 seconds. Throw in the Chinese greens stems and cook for 2 minutes, then add the leaves and toss. Stir in the chile jam and stir-fry for 2–3 minutes, or until the vegetables are cooked through but still crunchy. Add soy sauce if necessary.

vegetables with miso & sake

A dash of miso adds depth to this simple stir-fry. You'll find edamame, also called baby green soybeans, in the freezer section of the supermarket.

1 tablespoon vegetable oil
2 garlic cloves, crushed
6½ oz. sugar snap peas
6½ oz. baby zucchini, chopped into chunks on the diagonal
6½ oz. frozen edamame, defrosted
shoyu or tamari soy sauce, to taste (optional)

Sauce
2 heaping teaspoons red or brown miso paste
1 tablespoon mirin (Japanese rice wine)
1 tablespoon sake
⅔ cup dashi or vegetable stock
1 tablespoon cornstarch

Serves 4

Combine all the sauce ingredients in a bowl and set aside.

Heat the oil in a wok or large skillet until hot, then add the garlic and stir-fry over high heat for 30 seconds. Throw in the sugar snap peas and zucchini and stir-fry for 2–3 minutes. Add the edamame and toss well, then pour in the sauce. Bring to a boil, then reduce the heat and simmer, stirring occasionally, for about 3 minutes, or until the vegetables are cooked through but still crunchy.

Taste and add a dash of soy sauce if you think it needs it. Divide between 4 bowls and serve immediately.

eggplant with coconut, lemon grass, & cilantro

A jar of Thai red curry paste is one of a cook's most useful pantry staples. Here its fragrant, spicy flavors are used for a curry-like stir-fry.

2 tablespoons vegetable oil
1 onion, finely chopped
1 tablespoon Thai red curry paste
1 lb. 4 oz. eggplant, halved lengthwise and sliced ¼ inch thick
3 tomatoes, peeled, seeded, and chopped
2 tablespoons unsweetened canned coconut cream
½ cup coconut milk
1 tablespoon fish sauce, plus extra if needed
1 lemon grass stalk, outer skin removed and bottom 3 inches bruised
3 tablespoons roughly chopped cilantro leaves

Serves 4

Heat the oil in a wok or large skillet until hot. Add the onion and stir-fry over high heat for 2–3 minutes, or until softened and golden. Stir in the curry paste and cook for 30 seconds.

Add the eggplant and tomatoes and toss until well mixed. Stir in the coconut cream, coconut milk, fish sauce, and lemon grass. Reduce the heat and simmer for 5–6 minutes, or until the eggplant is tender. Taste and add more fish sauce if you think it needs it. Divide between 4 bowls and serve immediately.

Classic coleslaw is revamped here by replacing the mayonnaise with a Vietnamese-inspired peanut and lime dressing and by enhancing the shredded cabbage and carrot mix with crunchy bean sprouts and cilantro leaves. Remember not to toss the vegetables in the warm sauce until just before serving so that they don't lose their crunch.

warm tossed Asian coleslaw

1 tablespoon peanut oil

1 shallot, finely chopped

2 garlic cloves, finely chopped

1 large red chile, seeded and thinly sliced

1½ cups very thinly sliced white cabbage

1½ cups very thinly sliced red cabbage

1 large carrot, cut into very thin matchsticks

1 cup bean sprouts

a small bunch of cilantro, whole leaves only

Dressing

3 tablespoons crunchy peanut butter

2 teaspoons light brown sugar

1 tablespoon sesame oil

1 tablespoon peanut oil

2 tablespoons rice vinegar

1 tablespoon light soy sauce

freshly squeezed juice of 1 lime

Serves 4

Combine all the dressing ingredients with ½ cup water in a bowl and stir well until the sugar has dissolved.

Heat the oil in a wok or skillet until hot, then add the shallot, garlic, and chile. Stir-fry over high heat for 1 minute.

Add the dressing to the wok and bring to a boil, then reduce the heat and simmer gently until the dressing has thickened slightly.

When you are ready to serve the salad, put the white and red cabbage, carrot, bean sprouts, and cilantro in a serving bowl and pour in the warm dressing. Toss well and serve immediately.

meat

Pork tenderloin is given a spicy boost with classic Thai flavorings and the toasted coconut finishes off this super-tasty stir-fry perfectly. If you can't get hold of Thai sweet basil, simply replace with cilantro.

4–5 tablespoons grated fresh coconut (or desiccated, if necessary)

1 lb. 4 oz. pork tenderloin

2 tablespoons vegetable oil

1-inch piece of fresh ginger

3 garlic cloves, thinly sliced

4 whole bird's-eye chiles

1 lemon grass stalk, outer skin removed and bottom 2 inches bruised

1 tablespoon fish sauce

2 tablespoons chili sauce

a large handful of Thai sweet basil

sea salt and freshly ground black pepper

cooked rice or noodles, to serve

Serves 4

pork with chile, Thai sweet basil, & toasted coconut

Heat a wok or large skillet until hot. Add the coconut and dry-fry over high heat for a few minutes until golden. Remove from the wok and set aside.

Put the pork tenderloin between 2 large sheets of plastic wrap and hit with a rolling pin until you have flattened it to about 1 inch. Slice very thinly and season with sea salt and black pepper.

Heat the oil in a wok or large skillet until hot, then sear the pork in 2 or 3 batches over high heat, adding more oil if necessary. Remove the pork from the wok and set aside.

Add the ginger, garlic, chiles, and lemon grass to the wok and stir-fry for 1 minute. Return the pork to the wok and stir for 1 minute. Add the fish sauce and chili sauce and stir well. Cook for 2 minutes, or until the pork is completely cooked through. Remove from the heat and stir in the Thai sweet basil.

Divide between 4 bowls and serve immediately with rice or noodles, garnished with the toasted coconut.

A world away from the local takeout's greasy battered nuggets drowned in a fluorescent gloop, this scrumptious recipe uses lean pork tenderloin, wok-fried with cucumber wedges and juicy pineapple chunks and lightly coated in a sweet and tangy sauce.

sweet & sour pork with pineapple & cucumber

1 lb. 4 oz. pork tenderloin, cut into 1-inch chunks

1 tablespoon light soy sauce

2 teaspoons finely grated fresh ginger

2 tablespoons vegetable oil

1 large red bell pepper, seeded and cut into 1-inch chunks

1 large onion, cut into 8 wedges

½ large cucumber, roughly peeled, halved, seeded, and thickly sliced

10 oz. fresh or canned pineapple, cut into 1-inch chunks

cooked rice or noodles, to serve

Sauce

⅓ cup pure pineapple juice

¼ cup tomato ketchup

2 tablespoons rice vinegar

1 tablespoon light soy sauce

1 tablespoon sugar

1 tablespoon cornstarch

Serves 4

Combine all the sauce ingredients in a bowl and set aside.

Put the pork, soy sauce, and ginger in a bowl and mix well. Cover and marinate in the fridge for 20 minutes, if possible.

Heat the oil in a wok or large skillet until hot, then add the pork in batches (don't overcrowd the wok, otherwise the pork will stew rather than fry). Stir-fry over high heat for 4–5 minutes until nearly cooked through and well sealed all over. Remove the pork from the wok and set aside.

Throw the red bell pepper and onion into the wok and stir-fry for 2–3 minutes. Return the pork to the wok with any juices. Pour in the sauce and toss everything together. Bring to a boil, then reduce the heat. Add the cucumber and pineapple and simmer gently for 3–4 minutes, or until the sauce has thickened and the pork is cooked through. Divide between 4 bowls and serve immediately with rice or noodles.

Sweet, sticky, and finger-lickin' good, these irresistible orange-glazed beef strips make a great sharing dish for a dinner party. Serve them with crisp Little Gem lettuce leaves to make the perfect fingerfood wrappers.

14 oz. beef fillet

1 tablespoon light soy sauce

¼ cup cornstarch

vegetable oil, for frying

2 heads Little Gem or Boston lettuce, leaves separated

lime wedges, to serve

Sauce

2 garlic cloves, crushed

1 teaspoon finely grated fresh ginger

3 tablespoons dark soy sauce

grated zest of 1 large orange

⅓ cup freshly squeezed orange juice

¼ cup honey

1 heaping tablespoon tomato ketchup

Serves 4–6

sticky orange beef lettuce wraps

Put the beef in the freezer for 20 minutes, or until quite firm, then remove and cut into thin strips. Toss the beef in the soy sauce, then put in a freezer bag with the cornstarch. Seal the bag and give it a good shake so that all the beef strips are evenly coated.

Pour a 1-inch depth of oil in a wok and heat until hot. Add the beef in small batches, separating the strips with tongs to stop them sticking together. Cook for 2–3 minutes, or until browned and crisp. Remove with a slotted spoon and let drain on paper towels.

To make the sauce, pour away most of the oil from the wok, leaving about ½ tablespoon. Heat this gently, then add the garlic and ginger and stir-fry for 1 minute. Add the remaining sauce ingredients and bring to a boil. Let it bubble away briskly for 3 minutes, or until thickened.

Return the beef to the wok and cook for a few minutes until the sauce is sticky and clings to the beef. Remove from the heat.

Divide the beef between 4–6 plates and serve with the lettuce leaves and lime wedges. Wrap the beef in the leaves and enjoy!

Fragrant and mouth-tingling Szechuan peppercorns give a wonderful flavor and aroma to tender sirloin steak and sweet, creamy butternut squash. If you can't find Szechuan peppercorns in the spice section of your supermarket, visit your nearest Asian grocery store.

1 lb. 4 oz. sirloin steak, trimmed of fat and thinly sliced against the grain

14 oz. butternut squash flesh, diced

2 tablespoons peanut oil

2 garlic cloves, thinly sliced

1 tablespoon finely grated fresh ginger

3 tablespoons sweet chili sauce

2 tablespoons dark soy sauce

a small bunch of cilantro leaves, roughly chopped

½ red chile, seeded and thinly sliced, to garnish

Marinade

2 tablespoons dark soy sauce

1 tablespoon crushed Szechuan peppercorns

Serves 4–6

beef with butternut squash & Szechuan pepper

Combine the marinade ingredients in a bowl, stir in the beef, cover, and marinate in the fridge for 20–30 minutes.

Bring a saucepan of lightly salted water to a boil, then add the butternut squash. Bring back to a boil and blanch for about 5 minutes, or until tender, then drain well and set aside.

Heat the peanut oil in a wok or large skillet until hot. Add the beef and stir-fry over high heat for 3–4 minutes, or until sealed. Remove the beef from the wok and set aside.

Add the garlic and ginger to the wok and stir-fry for 3–4 minutes, or until golden. Add the butternut squash with the sweet chili sauce, soy sauce, and 1 tablespoon water. Bring to a boil, then reduce the heat and simmer gently for 2 minutes.

Return the beef to the wok and stir-fry until cooked through. Remove from the heat and stir in the chopped cilantro. Divide between 4–6 bowls and garnish with the sliced chile.

Tamarind fruits contain a soft, sticky pulp with a tart, mouth-puckering taste. The pulp is widely used in Asian cooking and is conveniently available in paste form in jars. In this recipe, toffee-like palm sugar balances the sour tamarind and gives a wonderful depth to the dish.

tamarind lamb with sugar snap peas

14 oz. lamb leg steaks, cut into 1-inch cubes

1½ tablespoons vegetable oil

1½ cups sugar snap peas

cooked rice, to serve

Marinade

2½ tablespoons tamarind paste

3 tablespoons freshly squeezed orange juice

2½ tablespoons palm sugar or dark brown sugar

1 teaspoon finely grated fresh ginger

1 red chile, seeded and finely chopped

1 garlic clove, crushed

½ teaspoon sea salt, plus extra if needed

Serves 2

Combine all the marinade ingredients in a non-metal bowl, stir in the lamb, cover, and marinate in the fridge for 30–60 minutes. Bring up to room temperature before cooking.

Remove the lamb from the bowl of marinade, letting any excess marinade drip from the meat back into the bowl. Heat the oil in a wok or large skillet until hot, then stir-fry the lamb in 2 or 3 batches over high heat until sealed all over. Return all the lamb to the wok, then reduce the heat and stir in the sugar snap peas.

Pour in the reserved marinade and simmer gently until the sugar snap peas are cooked through but still crunchy. Taste and add more salt if you think it needs it.

Divide between 2 bowls and serve with rice.

poultry

Ideal for quick and casual entertaining, this isn't just a routine stir-fry – the distinctive taste of yellow bean sauce and the colorful combination of red and yellow bell peppers make for a memorable dish.

2 large skinless chicken breasts, cut into 1-inch pieces

1 tablespoon peanut oil

1 red bell pepper, seeded and thinly sliced

1 yellow bell pepper, seeded and thinly sliced

2 tablespoons yellow bean sauce

½ tablespoon light soy sauce

⅓ cup chicken stock

2 teaspoons cornstarch

cooked rice tossed with toasted sesame oil, to serve

1 tablespoon slivered almonds, lightly toasted in a skillet, to garnish (optional)

Marinade

½ tablespoon Chinese rice wine or dry sherry

1 tablespoon light soy sauce

1 teaspoon toasted sesame oil

½ teaspoon sugar

1 teaspoon finely grated fresh ginger

a pinch of dried red pepper flakes

Serves 2

chicken with yellow bean sauce & rainbow peppers

Combine all the marinade ingredients in a bowl, then add the chicken pieces and mix well. Cover and marinate in the fridge for 10–15 minutes.

Heat the oil in a wok or large skillet until hot, then add the chicken and stir-fry over high heat for 3–4 minutes until golden, well sealed, and nearly cooked through. Remove from the wok and set aside.

Add the bell peppers to the wok and stir-fry over high heat for 2 minutes. Return the chicken to the wok and add the yellow bean sauce. Cook for 1 minute, stirring occasionally.

Meanwhile, combine the soy sauce, stock, and cornstarch in a bowl with 2 tablespoons cold water. Stir until smooth, then pour into the wok. Simmer gently until the sauce has thickened and the chicken is cooked through.

Divide between 2 bowls and serve with the oil-tossed rice. Sprinkle with slivered almonds, if using, to garnish.

Fresh lemon grass and kaffir lime leaves infuse this Vietnamese-style dish with a tantalizing citrus zing. Using skinless chicken thighs keeps the stir-fry moist without unnecessary fat and with the bone in you get lots more flavor from the chicken.

8 skinless chicken thighs (bone in), each cut into 3 with a sharp cleaver

2 tablespoons peanut oil

1 onion, very thinly sliced

3 bird's-eye chiles, chopped, plus extra, shredded, to garnish (optional)

3 tablespoons fish sauce

1 teaspoon sugar

cooked rice, to serve

lime wedges, to serve

3 scallions, green and light green parts only, thinly sliced on the diagonal, to garnish

Marinade

1 tablespoon finely grated fresh ginger

3 garlic cloves, crushed

3 lemon grass stalks, outer skin removed, cut into 1-inch pieces and well bruised

5 fresh kaffir lime leaves, torn to release their aroma

sea salt

Serves 4

Vietnamese fried chicken

Combine the marinade ingredients in a bowl with a good sprinkling of salt. Stir in the chicken, cover, and marinate in the fridge for 20–30 minutes.

Heat the oil in a wok or skillet pan until very hot, then add the chicken in 2 batches. Stir-fry over high heat for 5 minutes, or until the chicken is golden all over. Remove the chicken from the wok and set aside.

Add the onion and chiles to the wok and stir-fry for 1 minute. Return all the chicken to the wok with the fish sauce and sugar and toss everything together. Reduce the heat and continue to stir-fry for 5 minutes, or until the chicken is cooked through. Taste and add more fish sauce if you think it needs it.

Divide between 4 bowls and serve with rice and lime wedges. Garnish with the scallions and shredded chiles, if using.

Classic Peking duck is given an updated twist. Fresh plums mingle with slices of succulent duck dry-rubbed with aromatic five-spice powder in this original stir-fry.

2 skinless duck breasts, thinly sliced

1 teaspoon Chinese five-spice powder

2 tablespoons vegetable or peanut oil

1 onion, sliced

1 small eggplant, quartered and sliced

2 plums, pitted and cut into wedges

sea salt and freshly ground black pepper

cooked egg noodles, to serve

Sauce

3 tablespoons Chinese plum sauce

1 tablespoon rice vinegar

2 tablespoons honey

1 tablespoon dark soy sauce, plus extra if needed

Serves 2–3

five-spice duck with eggplant & plums

Combine all the sauce ingredients in a bowl and set aside.

Put the duck in a bowl and sprinkle over the five-spice powder and a pinch of sea salt and black pepper. Rub into the duck.

Heat the oil in a wok or large skillet until hot. Add the duck in batches and stir-fry over high heat until sealed all over. Remove the duck from the wok and set aside.

Add the onion to the wok, with a little more oil if necessary, and stir-fry for 2 minutes, or until softened and golden. Add the eggplant with a good sprinkling of water and stir-fry for 2–3 minutes. Return the duck to the wok and stir well. Pour in the sauce, reduce the heat, and simmer for 3–4 minutes, covered, until the eggplant is just tender.

Remove the lid, then stir in the plums and cook for 2 minutes. Add more salt or soy sauce if you think it needs it. Divide between 2–3 bowls and serve with egg noodles.

Why order out when you can knock out this fresh-tasting, healthy take on the perennial Chinese favorite quickly and easily? Don't worry if you can't find Chinese rice wine; simply substitute with dry sherry.

4 skinless chicken breasts, cut into thin strips

1 tablespoon sesame seeds

2 tablespoons peanut or vegetable oil

1 onion, thinly sliced

2 scallions, green parts only, thinly sliced or shredded, to garnish

cooked rice noodles, to serve

Marinade

1 tablespoon light soy sauce

1 tablespoon Chinese rice wine or dry sherry

2 teaspoons finely grated fresh ginger

2 garlic cloves, crushed

1 teaspoon cornstarch

Sauce

⅓ cup chicken stock

freshly squeezed juice and finely grated zest of 1 large unwaxed lemon

3 tablespoons honey

1 tablespoon light soy sauce

1 teaspoon toasted sesame oil

2 teaspoons cornstarch

Serves 4

lemon chicken with toasted sesame seeds

Combine all the marinade ingredients in a bowl, stir in the chicken, cover, and marinate in the fridge for 20–30 minutes.

Meanwhile, to make the sauce, put all the ingredients in a bowl with 2 tablespoons cold water, stir to combine, and set aside.

Heat a wok or large skillet until hot, then add the sesame seeds and stir over medium heat for about 2 minutes, or until lightly toasted. Remove from the wok and set aside.

Heat 1½ tablespoons of the oil in the wok until very hot. Add the chicken in 2 batches and stir-fry over high heat for 3–4 minutes until golden brown and well sealed all over. Remove the chicken from the wok and set aside.

Add the remaining oil to the wok and throw in the onion. Stir-fry for 2–3 minutes until softened and golden. Pour in the sauce and bring to a boil, then reduce the heat and simmer for 1 minute.

Return the chicken to the wok and stir through the sauce. Simmer for 2 minutes, or until the chicken is cooked through.

Divide between 4 bowls and serve with rice noodles. Sprinkle over the toasted sesame seeds and garnish with the scallions.

fish & seafood

Capturing the fine balance of hot, sweet, and sour flavors of Southeast Asian cuisine, this exotic salad makes for a refreshing opener or a light meal in itself.

warm shrimp, mango, & lychee salad

16 uncooked large shrimp, shelled but tails intact

2 teaspoons fish sauce, plus extra to taste (optional)

1 tablespoon peanut oil

½ large red chile, seeded and finely chopped

1 teaspoon tamarind paste

1 heaping tablespoon palm sugar or light brown sugar

freshly squeezed juice and grated zest of 1 unwaxed lime

½ ripe, large mango, peeled and cut into 1-inch chunks

12 fresh lychees, peeled, pitted, and halved

2 large handfuls of baby arugula

sea salt and freshly ground black pepper

Serves 4 as an appetizer or 2 as an entrée

Combine the shrimp, fish sauce, and some black pepper in a bowl.

Heat the oil in a wok or large skillet until hot. Add the shrimp and stir-fry over high heat for 2 minutes, or until the shrimp are opaque and cooked through. Remove the shrimp from the wok and set aside.

Add the chile to the wok and stir-fry over high heat for 30 seconds, or until just softened. Reduce the heat, then add the tamarind paste and palm sugar and stir until the sugar has dissolved. Remove from the heat and add the lime juice and zest and a pinch of sea salt or drizzle of fish sauce, to taste. Return the shrimp to the wok and carefully stir in the mango and lychees.

Divide the salad between 4 or 2 plates, scatter over the arugula, and toss gently.

This is a great prepare-ahead weekday supper—simply marinate the salmon with a gingery, honeyed teriyaki sauce the night before, then stir-fry with crunchy bok choy for a nutritious and delicious meal in under 15 minutes.

1 ½ lbs. skinless salmon fillet, cut into 1-inch pieces

1 tablespoon vegetable oil

3 scallions, white and light green parts only, thinly sliced on the diagonal

12 oz. baby bok choy, leaves thickly sliced and stalks thinly sliced

cooked rice or noodles, to serve

Marinade

1 tablespoon finely grated fresh ginger

3 tablespoons shoyu or tamari soy sauce (or light soy sauce)

3 tablespoons mirin (Japanese rice wine)

2 tablespoons honey

Serves 4

quick-fried teriyaki salmon with bok choy

Combine all the marinade ingredients in a bowl, then add the salmon pieces and mix well. Cover and marinate in the fridge overnight, if possible, or for 10–15 minutes.

Heat the oil in a wok or large skillet until hot, then add the salmon in 2 batches—shake off as much marinade as possible and reserve the marinade. Stir-fry the salmon over high heat for about 3 minutes, stirring occasionally, until sealed all over but the inside is still a little pink. Remove the salmon from the wok and set aside.

Add the scallions to the wok and stir-fry for 30 seconds. Add the bok choy and stir-fry for 1 minute, then add the reserved marinade and cook for 1 minute, stirring, until the leaves have just wilted and the stalks are cooked through but still crunchy. Return the salmon to the wok and gently stir through.

Divide between 4 bowls and serve with rice or noodles.

Pungent black bean sauce pairs beautifully with the subtle taste of cod in this simple, authentic recipe. Remember not to be too heavy-handed with the black bean sauce, as a little goes a long way. Feel free to substitute the cod with any other firm white fish.

cod with black bean sauce

1 tablespoon peanut oil

1 shallot, thinly sliced

2 garlic cloves, thinly sliced

1-inch piece of fresh ginger, peeled and shredded

2 scallions, thinly sliced, white and green parts kept separately

1½ tablespoons black bean sauce

⅓ cup fish stock

1 teaspoon sugar

12 oz. cod fillets, cut into 1¼-inch pieces

cooked rice, to serve

1 teaspoon toasted sesame oil, to serve

Serves 2

Heat the oil in a wok or large skillet until hot, then add the shallot, garlic, ginger, and white parts of the scallions. Stir-fry over high heat for 2 minutes, then stir in the black bean sauce.

Pour in the stock, along with the sugar, and bring to a boil. Simmer rapidly for 2 minutes until thickened, then reduce the heat and add the cod. Cook for about 3 minutes, stirring occasionally, until the fish is cooked through.

Divide between 2 bowls and serve with rice. Drizzle over the sesame oil and garnish with the green parts of the scallions.

A plate of crispy fried squid can be very satisfying indeed, but spike it with fiery chiles, fresh green peppercorns, and zesty galangal, as in this recipe, and it soon becomes a sensational meal, perfect for effortless entertaining.

wok-fried crispy squid with green peppercorns

3 garlic cloves, thinly sliced

1-inch piece of galangal (or ginger), peeled and thinly sliced

1 large red chile, seeded and shredded

2 sprigs of fresh green peppercorns

2 tablespoons fish sauce

1 teaspoon sugar

freshly squeezed juice of ½ lime

cooked rice or a green salad, to serve

lime wedges, to serve

Crispy squid

14 oz. cleaned squid, tentacles cut into bite-size pieces; body lightly scored on one side in a criss-cross pattern and cut into bite-size squares

2 teaspoons fish sauce

¾ cup all-purpose flour, seasoned with ¼ teaspoon cayenne pepper

vegetable oil, for frying

Serves 2

To make the crispy squid, toss the squid in the fish sauce. Put half the flour in a large freezer bag with half the squid. Seal the bag and give it a good shake so that the squid is evenly coated. Toss the squid into a colander and shake well to remove the excess flour. Set aside. Repeat with the remaining squid and flour.

Pour a 1-inch depth of oil in a wok or large skillet and heat until very hot (a small cube of bread dropped into the oil should brown in 20 seconds). Drop in the squid in 2 or 3 batches and cook for about 2 minutes, or until the squid pieces are golden all over. Remove with a slotted spoon and leave to drain on paper towels.

Pour away most of the oil from the wok, leaving only ½ tablespoon. Add the garlic, galangal, chile, and peppercorn sprigs and stir-fry over high heat for 1 minute. Return the squid to the wok along with the fish sauce and sugar and toss for 1 minute.

Remove from the heat and stir in the lime juice. Divide between 2 bowls and serve with rice or a green salad and lime wedges on the side.

sides

coconut rice

2½ cups basmati rice
1¾ cups coconut milk
sea salt

Serves 4

Wash the rice thoroughly in cold running water and drain well. Put in a saucepan.

Combine 2½ cups water, the coconut milk, and a pinch of sea salt in a bowl and pour into the pan with the rice. Set over medium heat and bring to a boil. Reduce the heat and simmer very gently until all the liquid has been absorbed.

Remove from the heat, cover, and let stand for 5 minutes before stirring gently to fluff up the rice grains. Serve immediately.

egg fried rice

2 tablespoons peanut or vegetable oil
2 garlic cloves, crushed
¾ cup frozen peas
4 cups cold, cooked jasmine rice
3 eggs, lightly beaten
2 tablespoons light soy sauce, plus extra if needed
2 teaspoons toasted sesame oil
sea salt and freshly ground black pepper

Serves 4

Heat the oil in a wok or large skillet until very hot, then add the garlic and stir-fry over high heat for 1 minute. Throw in the peas and cook for a further minute.

Add the rice to the wok and stir, breaking up any lumps.

Season the beaten eggs with a pinch of sea salt and black pepper. Make a well in the center of the wok and pour in the eggs. When the bottom starts to set, scramble the eggs with a wooden spoon until softly set in light, fluffy curds, then stir through the rice. Stir in the soy sauce and sesame oil. Taste and add a little more soy sauce or sea salt if you think it needs it.

lemon grass & kaffir lime jasmine rice

1¾ cups jasmine rice
1 lemon grass stalk
1-inch piece of fresh ginger, peeled and grated
3 kaffir lime leaves, torn to release their aroma

Serves 4

Wash the rice thoroughly in cold running water and drain well. Put in a saucepan with 2½ cups water.

Bruise or roughly crush the lemon grass and ginger with the back of a large knife or a pestle, then throw into the saucepan with the lime leaves. Stir well, then set the pan over medium heat. Bring to a boil, then reduce the heat, cover, and cook gently for about 15–18 minutes, or until all the liquid has been absorbed and the rice is just tender.

Remove from the heat and let stand, covered, for 5–10 minutes before serving.

spiced pilaf

1¾ cups basmati rice
1½ tablespoons vegetable oil
1 large onion, very thinly sliced
2 star anise
1 large cinnamon stick, broken in half
4 cardamom pods, crushed
⅔ cup unsalted cashews
sea salt

Serves 4

Wash the rice in cold running water and drain well. Set aside.

Heat 1 teaspoon of the oil in a skillet until hot, then add the onion. Cook over medium heat for 5–7 minutes, or until browned and soft. Add the spices and cook for 30 seconds. Add the rice and stir briefly to coat in the oil and onion. Remove from the heat and transfer everything to a saucepan. Add 2¼ cups water and a pinch of salt and bring to a boil. Reduce the heat and simmer very gently for 15–20 minutes, or until cooked. Remove from the heat, cover, and leave for 5 minutes.

Heat the remaining oil in a skillet until hot, then add the cashews. Toss until golden, then stir into the rice. Remove the whole spices, if desired, before serving.

mixed rice with macadamia nuts

1¼ cups brown basmati rice
½ cup wild rice
1 cup macadamia nuts
1 teaspoon toasted sesame oil
½ teaspoon Chinese five-spice powder
¼ teaspoon ground red chile
sea salt

Serves 2

Preheat the oven to 400°F.

Wash the rice thoroughly in cold running water and drain well. Put in a saucepan with 2¾ cups water and a pinch of salt. Bring to a boil, then reduce the heat and simmer very gently until all the water has been absorbed. Remove from the heat, cover, and leave for 10 minutes.

Put the macadamia nuts in a bowl and sprinkle over the oil. Mix thoroughly until well coated. Stir in the spices and ¼ teaspoon salt. Put on a baking sheet on a shelf near the top of the preheated oven and roast for 10–15 minutes, or until lightly toasted. Remove from the oven and leave for 2–3 minutes before stirring into the rice.

lemon & lentil rice

2¼ cups basmati rice
½ teaspoon ground turmeric
2 tablespoons vegetable oil
5 tablespoons yellow split lentils
1 teaspoon fennel seeds
1 teaspoon mustard seeds
freshly squeezed juice of 1 large lemon
sea salt

Serves 4–6

Wash the rice thoroughly in cold running water and drain well. Put in a saucepan with 2⅔ cups water, the turmeric, and a pinch of salt. Bring to a boil, then reduce the heat and simmer gently for 15 minutes, or until all the water has been absorbed. Remove from the heat.

Heat the oil in a wok or skillet until hot, then add the lentils and stir-fry over high heat until golden. Stir in the fennel seeds and cook until they start to sizzle. Stir in the mustard seeds and when they start to pop remove the wok from the heat. Add the rice and lemon juice to the wok, then mix well until thoroughly combined. Taste and add a little salt if you think it needs it.

sesame soba noodles

6½ oz. dried soba noodles
1½ teaspoons white sesame seeds
2 teaspoons toasted sesame oil
1 teaspoon shoyu or tamari soy sauce
1½ teaspoons black sesame seeds

Serves 2

Bring a saucepan of water to a boil. Throw in the noodles and gently push into the water as they soften. Cook for 4–5 minutes, or according to the package instructions. Drain well and transfer to a large bowl.

Toast the white sesame seeds in a dry skillet over medium heat until golden.

Add the oil and soy sauce to the bowl of noodles and toss well. Sprinkle over the toasted white and black sesame seeds and mix until evenly dispersed.

soy & scallion egg noodles

1½ tablespoons vegetable oil
1 garlic clove, crushed
4 scallions, thinly sliced, white and green parts kept separately
1 lb. 4 oz. fresh thin egg noodles
2 tablespoons light soy sauce

Serves 4

Heat the oil in a wok or large skillet until hot, then add the garlic and white parts of the scallions. Stir-fry over high heat for 30 seconds.

Throw in the noodles and toss well. Sprinkle over 1½ tablespoons of the soy sauce and 2 tablespoons water and stir-fry over high heat for 3–4 minutes, or until the noodles are cooked through. Taste and add the remaining soy sauce if you think it needs it. Remove from the heat and stir through the green parts of the scallions.

egg noodles with sweet chili & lime

10 oz. fresh medium egg noodles
½ teaspoon toasted sesame oil
½ tablespoon peanut oil
1 garlic clove, crushed
1 red chile, seeded and very thinly sliced
2 tablespoons sweet chili sauce
½ teaspoon sugar
finely grated zest of 1 lime
freshly squeezed juice of ½ lime
1½ tablespoons finely chopped cilantro leaves

Serves 2

Cook the noodles according to the package instructions, then drain well and toss with the sesame oil.

Heat the oil in a wok or large skillet until hot. Add the garlic and red chile and stir-fry over high heat for 30 seconds. Stir in the chili sauce, sugar, lime zest, and juice, then stir in the noodles and chopped cilantro.

index

conversion chart

Volume equivalents:

American	Metric	Imperial
6 tbsp butter	85 g	3 oz.
7 tbsp butter	100 g	3½ oz.
1 stick butter	115 g	4 oz.
1 teaspoon	5 ml	
1 tablespoon	15 ml	
¼ cup	60 ml	2 fl.oz.
⅓ cup	75 ml	2½ fl.oz.
½ cup	125 ml	4 fl.oz.
⅔ cup	150 ml	5 fl.oz. (¼ pint)
¾ cup	175 ml	6 fl.oz.
1 cup	250 ml	8 fl.oz.

Oven temperatures:

170°C	(325°F)	Gas 3
180°C	(350°F)	Gas 4
190°C	(375°F)	Gas 5
200°C	(400°F)	Gas 6
220°C	(425°F)	Gas 8

Weight equivalents:

Imperial	Metric
1 oz.	30 g
2 oz.	55 g
3 oz.	85 g
3½ oz.	100 g
4 oz.	115 g
5 oz.	140 g
6 oz.	175 g
8 oz. (½ lb.)	225 g
9 oz.	250 g
10 oz.	280 g
11½ oz.	325 g
12 oz.	350 g
13 oz.	375 g
14 oz.	400 g
15 oz.	425 g
16 oz. (1 lb.)	450 g

Measurements:

Inches	Cm
¼ inch	0.5 cm
½ inch	1 cm
¾ inch	1.5 cm
1 inch	2.5 cm
2 inches	5 cm
3 inches	7 cm
4 inches	10 cm
5 inches	12 cm
6 inches	15 cm
7 inches	18 cm
8 inches	20 cm
9 inches	23 cm
10 inches	25 cm
11 inches	28 cm
12 inches	30 cm